ANOTHER BOOK WITHOUT PICTURES

BY: DR. MARV NELSON

Another Book Without Pictures

By Dr. Marv Nelson

Another Book Without Pictures
2025 by Dr. Marv Nelson

Published by Candor Press

This is another book

without any pictures

But...trust me, it's still
going to be fun...

Don't believe me?

Just watch...

The person reading this
has gotten themselves
into a pickle...

They have to read every
word, on every page!

WHAT!?

Even if it reads: "I eat spaghetti with my feet"

Or: "My nickname is booger eater" because, yeah, I eat BOOGERS!

Wait a second, no I don't!

Please, I don't want to
say these words, can I
shut the book and stop!?

NO!?

Well, my feet are so **HAIRY**, you can't see my **TOENAILS**!

That's not true!

No don't believe what I am saying!

Wait, yes they are and sometimes, I braid my

OK, this is getting out of hand!

Do I still have to read??

WWWG

WH

THIS ISN

GGHHH.

Y!?!?

I'T FAIR!!!

Yes it is!
Let me sing you a song!

"I'm a fuzzy, fuzzy
everywhere, even
and I don't

bear, I eat bugs from my hair, care!"

NO. I. DON'T!

YES. I. DO.

You are the greatest **KID** ever to be born, because you asked me to read this book!

You are smart, funny and tricky!

The person reading this is
the weirdest person alive!

They love to call
themselves...

TOOTING TOM,

because they are always tooting, and it smells **BAD!**

THIS. IS. NOT. TRUE!

Umm...actually it is!

OH MAN, please let me stop this silliness! I'm getting embarrassed...can I PLEASE STOP!?

NO!?

Well, now I am going to shout:

I AM AN ALIEN WHO SHOOTS LASERS FROM MY HAIRY ARMPITS!

What!? Who says this stuff!?

Did YOU write
this!?

Can I stop now!?

I DO NOT WANT TO STOP. DON'T LET ME!

Yes I do! No I don't!

My favorite thing to do is make **silly sounds**!

No it's not!

You picked the right book kids because now I have to say super silly things like:

Oh no...here it comes...

ARRRRRRGH BUUUU

TOOOOOOTTTYYY

BORK OOO

AHHHHHHHH GO

EATER! IEEEEEEE

UUUURP

OOOOO

OOOOOOOBER

EEEEEEEEEEEEEE

WHAT IS HAPPENING TO ME!? Am I going crazy!?

Can this wild ride end!?

My nose is a

giant

strawberry

strudel!

Huh!? That's not true at all.

Well, maybe it is. What do you think?

Don't answer that.

Actually, answer it. Tell me my nose is a **giant strawberry strudel**

Did you know
this was going to
happen to me!?

You did!?

I knew it!

OK, I think I'm running out of steam here.

Hopefully the silliness is over.

Would you like that?

NO!?

Oh, come on!

Well, I guess now I need to say:

LALALALALALA

ZOINKOOINKO

POO POO BUTT

OINK OINK I'm a

PIGGY!

I am definitely
not!

I have to be
done.

THE. END.

Now, I'll read it again!

Umm...SIKE!

Do you want me to read it again?

Say NO, OK?

TRULY. THE. END.

A whole new look at children's books without pictures. Take a wild, and crazy ride as you read this book to your kids. Enjoy their laughter...at YOUR EXPENSE!

WARNING: Your children will laugh and laugh as you are forced to read EVERY word on every page!

Dr. Marv Nelson is a father, teacher and pastor who lives to write serious (and not so serious) books.

ISBN 979-889704112-1